# Smuggling
# and other transgressions in the South Hams, Devon.

By Brian Wigley

ORCHARD PUBLICATIONS
2 Orchard Close, Chudleigh, Devon TQ13 0LR
Telephone: (01626) 852714

ISBN 1 898964 57 2

*Printed by*
Hedgerow Print, Crediton, Devon EX17 1ES

# CONTENTS

Preface   1

The Smuggler's Song   2

1. The South Hams   3

2 Why Smuggle?   4

3 Organisation and Practice   7

4 The Revenue Men   10

5 Coves and Caves
(Dartmouth Castle to Salcombe Estuary)   13

6 Coves and Caves
(Salcombe Estuary to the River Yealm)   20

7 The Present Day   30

8 Wrecking   32

9 Pirates   34

Appendix 1
Burgh Island - a brief history   37

Appendix 2
Bronze Age palstave mould   39

Appendix 3
The River Erme.   39

# PREFACE

Much has been written about smuggling, particularly smuggling in the West Country of Britain. But it appears that for some reason, nothing has so far been published specifically about smuggling in that very special part of Devon known as the South Hams. This book aims to rectify that by taking the reader on a walk along the coastal path from Dartmouth Castle to the River Yealm and considering the history, legend, rumour, conjecture and fact on the way.

This part of the county is now a mecca for tourists, and visitors from other parts of the country find a certain romance in drinking a pint of local cider in a 17th or 18th century inn which claims to have been a smuggler's haunt. And whilst no one is saying that inn keepers exaggerate their histories to attract tourists, care has to be taken in sorting out fact from fiction. Help in doing this has been given by Plymouth Museums and Art Gallery, The Devon Study Library with their newspaper archives, Exeter Archaeological Unit, HM Customs and Excise, Exeter, and a number of elderly Devonians, some of whom remember conversations with grandparents and great-grandparents giving a flavour of what it was like to live in a coastal community during the violent times in the 19th century.

If you intend to use this book as a walking guide, take your time and savour the beauty and the atmosphere of the area, and the centuries of history that has preceded you. (Above Seacombe Sand you can see a Prehistoric field system). But above all, enjoy this most beautiful stretch of coastline which reveals a new secret each time you walk it.

Brian Wigley


Foot Note: *Whether you are walking the path or browsing in the comfort of your living room, you will find a large scale Ordnance Survey Outdoor Leisure 20 map of South Devon a useful aid. Also, if you are walking be warned, this stretch of the coast path is rugged and remote and walking boots and weather proof clothing are necessary. Also in certain bays and coves the tide moves quickly and your only way of escape can easily be cut off. Nevertheless - enjoy.*

# The Smuggler's Song by Rudyard Kipling

If you wake at midnight, and hear a horse's feet,
Don't go drawing back the blind, or looking in the street,
Them that asks no questions isn't told a lie.
Watch the wall, my darling, while the Gentlemen go by!

> *Five-and-twenty ponies,*
> *Trotting through the dark -*
> *Brandy for the Parson,*
> *'Baccy for the Clerk;*
> *Laces for a lady, letters for a spy,*
> *And watch the wall, my darling, while the Gentlemen go by!*

Running round the woodlump if you chance to find
Little barrels, roped and tarred, all full of brandy wine.
Don't you shout to come and look, nor take 'em for your play;
Put the brushwood back again, and they'll be gone next day!

If you see the stable door setting open wide;
If you see a tired horse lying down inside;
If your mother mends a coat cut about and tore;
If the linings wet and warm - don't you ask no more!

If you meet King George's men, dressed in blue and red,
You be careful what you say, and mindful what is said.
If they call you 'pretty maid,' and chuck you 'neath the chin,
Don't you tell where no one is, nor yet where no one's been!

Knocks and footsteps round the house - whistles after dark -
You've no call for running out till the house-dogs bark.
Trusty's here, and Pincher's here, and see how dumb they lie -
They don't fret or follow when the Gentlemen go by!
If you do as you've been told, likely there's a chance
You'll be give a dainty doll, all the way from France,
With a cap of Valenciennes, and a velvet hood -
A present from the Gentlemen, along o' being good!

> *Five-and-twenty ponies,*
> *Trotting through the dark -*
> *Brandy for the Parson,*
> *'Baccy for the Clerk.*
> *Them that asks no questions isn't told a lie -*
> *Watch the wall my darling, while the Gentlemen go by!*

2

# 1   THE SOUTH HAMS

The South Hams is an area of Devon which is east of Plymouth, west of the River Dart, and south of Dartmoor. Before the coming of the railway and modern road links it would have been exceedingly remote and very difficult for the military and the excise men to supervise. The coastline is rugged and beautiful with numerous small beaches and coves. The River Yealm forms the western border of the South Hams, the River Dart the eastern boundary and roughly half way between the two, the Salcombe Estuary gives access from the sea not only to Kingsbridge, but to a number of small villages and hamlets along several creeks which lead off the main estuary.

The coastline has changed little over many centuries and a walk along the Devon coast path today can easily stimulate the imagination to the point where it is almost possible to hear the keel of a boat scrape ashore in one of the coves and see ghostly figures carrying barrels of brandy up the beach to a cave in the cliff. Even the path you are walking on was almost certainly the path along which the contraband would have been carried to a safe house. Most villages, especially those close to the sea, boast an inn, a house or even a church, where booty is alleged to have been hidden, but the question is, are these claims made to satisfy the needs of tourists who crave for a dramatic story, or can they be substantiated? There is no doubt that smuggling was carried out in the South Hams, but much of the 'evidence' is based on myth and legend and is often contradictory. So, any reliable records of that evidence are difficult to find and sparse in the extreme and research suggests that nothing has been written specifically about smuggling in the South Hams.

But the South Hams by the very nature of its remoteness and its geology is ideally suited for nefarious activity — modern day smugglers realise this and certainly take advantage of it. Where then is the evidence for smuggling in the 17th, 18th and 19th centuries to be found, and is the shortage of evidence simply due to the fact that smuggling was not a major occupation of the time, or because the geographical nature of the area made it easy to get away with it and it remained unrecorded.

True evidence cannot be found in legend and myth. Much of this will have been passed verbally from one family to another and from one generation to the next. Inevitably the story will have developed in the telling, and whilst it cannot be relied upon as absolute truth, it can certainly give pointers with regard to individual people and locations which can guide further research.

Another item of evidence which does not seem to have been researched thus far is the caves along the South Hams coastline. Yes, they have been identified as storage sites for contraband, but is that stating the obvious? What is not so obvious is the origin of the names they have been given. But first, let's consider another question, why smuggle?

3

Until the beginning of the 14th century, all trade out of and into England was free and unencumbered. However, during the reign of Edward 1, customs duty was placed on all wool exports. Such was the demand for wool in Europe that, although initially, the duty was quite small, merchants sought out those ports, beaches and coves which were not attended by the excise men to ship out their merchandise unencumbered by tax. If caught however, the penalties were severe and in 1661, anyone convicted of the illegal exporting of wool could be sentenced to death. So, smugglers armed themselves and to attempt to control the situation, Charles II created the Board of Customs in 1661, which, in turn, could call upon the army for support.

Wool is by no means the first or the only export of goods from the area. There is evidence of the export of tin from Devon and Cornwall to the Mediterranean countries from before the Roman occupation. Tin was essential to the making of bronze and as such was highly sought after and at one time it was believed that Cornwall had the exclusive claim on tin production. The discovery of a Bronze Age wreck off the coast of Devon, or at least its cargo and stone anchors, makes it necessary to take a new and serious look at the history of the tin trade in Devon. It is now known that tin mining was carried out extensively on Dartmoor. Is the Devon wreck evidence that the tin was brought down from the Moor, perhaps along the River Avon and the River Erme, and maybe even converted into ingots near the coast, then shipped out from a convenient estuary mooring — of which there are many along this coast.

The remains of the wreck in question were discovered at the mouth of the River Erme — all that was left of her cargo being forty two irregularly shaped ingots of almost pure tin, the largest weighing almost 13 kilos. If, as is suspected, the tin from the mines on Dartmoor was brought to the coast by way of the Avon and Erme, the question has to be asked 'Where would the most natural storage site be and the most convenient place to load the ships of traders?' The immediate response is Burgh Island. The island is situated immediately opposite the point where the Avon meets the sea and would be the perfect spot and the Erme is only a short distance to the west. In support of this, The Revd. Sabine Baring-Gould makes an interesting observation in his book '*Devon*' published in 1899:

> '*Above where the River Erme debouches into the sea is Oldaport, the remains, supposed to be Roman, of a harbour commanded by two towers. The ancient port occupying two creeks remains silted up. There is absolutely no record of its having been used in mediaeval times, and this leads to the supposition that it is considerably earlier.*'

But more about Burgh Island later.

The unrestricted export of tin went on for centuries until, in the early 14th century, the Duchy of Cornwall was given the right to buy all tin which came up for sale. All ingots had to be taken to one of the Stannary towns to be tested for quality and stamped. This obviously had a controlling effect on the price since the Duchy were not inclined to negotiate. Many traders therefore, carried on as before, and regular cargoes of undeclared ingots of tin were shipped out hidden under other goods, often barrels of pilchards. But because of this avoidance, laws both increased and became more severe. It is perhaps no wonder that the people involved in ignoring them were known as 'free-traders'. They were also known as 'owlers' because of the calls they made to communicate with one another.

So far we have only considered smuggling in terms of taking goods out of the country whereas most people consider it to be bringing illicit goods in. And it is in this role that smuggling gained its romantic, almost respectable reputation.

From Elizabethan times up to the middle of the 19th century, smuggling could almost be described as a social service. In the working classes and the peasantry there was, by the standards of today, abject poverty. Even in the lower ranks of the aspiring semi-skilled workers, luxuries, such as those available to their masters were denied to them because of the high taxes imposed on their import. An example of this is found in G.M. Trevelyan's book, 'English Social History'. He writes:

*'In the 16th century, tobacco played a great part in English colonial and commercial expansion and in the trade of Bristol. There were as yet no English colonies, but already in 1597 the new American weed was being smuggled into the creeks of the West Country on a large scale...in open and armed defiance of the custom house officers. The habit of taking tobacco in long clay pipes was very general by the time the Queen died.'*

Admittedly it cannot be argued that tobacco is one of life's essential requirements. But this is not what smuggling was about. Smuggling provided the luxuries of life that, if bought legitimately, were well beyond the pockets of ordinary people. Trevelyan goes on to write:

*'...in Charles II's reign thousands of well-to-do Londoners frequented the 'coffee-houses', to enjoy the fashionable new drinks brought over by the East India Company. By early in the reign of George III all classes in town and country were drinking tea in their own homes. The poor sweetened the bitter herb with large quantities of sugar. Until the younger Pitt reduced the high duties, the scale on which smuggling was carried on was prodigious. In 1784 Pitt calculated that thirteen million pounds of tea were consumed in the Kingdom, of which only five and a half million had paid duty.'*

Two examples of luxuries which could not have been enjoyed by ordinary people without the intervention of the smuggling fraternity and Trevelyan gives this example of how smuggling was seen in the community.

*'Smuggling added to the interest of people's lives almost as much as poaching, and was regarded as equally innocent. Parson Woodforde, a truly good as well as respectable man, wrote on March 29th, 1777: "Andrews the smuggler brought me this night about 11 o'clock a bagg of Hyson tea, 6 pound in weight. He frightened us just a little by whistling under the parlour window just as we were going to bed. I gave him some Geneva and paid him for the tea at 10/6 per pound." The inhabitants of this inland rectory thought and spoke of 'Andrews the smuggler' just as one might speak of Andrews the grocer!'*

Smuggling was, of course, not limited to tobacco and tea. Huge quantities of brandy and other spirits were brought into the country by routes which by-passed the excise men. Also, no matter how those who benefited from the trade viewed the smugglers, they did not carry out their activities to improve the standard of living of their customers. They made massive profits from their so-called 'free trading'. So much so that if only one in three of their trips was successful, it was financially worth doing.

The answer to the question 'Why smuggling?' therefore is double barrelled. It provided luxuries for those people who had the right contacts and at a much more reasonable price than the legitimate market would have to charge to cover the payment of tax. It also kept a relatively large number of people in a lucrative, if sometimes hazardous occupation.

It might perhaps be thought that smuggling was an activity carried out by two or three men in a small fishing boat who brought contraband into a remote cove on a dark night, hid it in a cave until the coast was clear and then sold it to the local populace. This was no doubt true on some occasions and especially before some sophistication came into the process. However, in reality, each run would be carefully planned and executed and groups of men and women were formed, each with varied responsibilities to make as certain as could be that things went smoothly and efficiently. These groups would sometimes be made up of individual families who had particular skills, facilities or, importantly, contacts — direct or indirect — with the excise men.

The trip from the continent was frequently made by a boat which, because of its size, would be unable to come close inshore. These boats could be as large as 300 tons and would, particularly as the customs service became more organised, be armed, and ready to fight. They would be met at a prearranged point by one or more boats rowed out from the shore and the cargo transferred. Meanwhile, the other organising groups would be at work.

Look-outs would make certain that the landing area and its surrounds was clear of excise men or, even worse, troops. If there was any danger of an ambush, an agreed signal would be given to the boats at sea. At night this might be by means of a spout lantern. These were specially made lanterns fitted with a spout which enabled the light to be accurately directed towards the boats and not be seen elsewhere. During the day signals warning of excise-men were many and various. The look-out might walk along the cliff path singing an agreed song. Or someone might ride a horse in a particular direction wearing a shirt of a certain colour. The possibilities were, of course, endless. In the villages some of the houses and cottages had — and some still have — small pointed windows in which a candle would be lit if the revenue men were about. When warnings were given, the boats would either stand off or take shelter in a nearby cove until the all-clear was given.

Assuming that there were no delays for security reasons, the transportation group would have arrived at a convenient meeting point with horses or mules. Sometimes there could be as many as a hundred or more animals involved, and with the men and women supervising the horses, it could not be considered an unobtrusive operation. Many of the beaches and coves in the South Hams used for landing smuggled goods were, and still are, difficult to get to by land. The nearest road might be two or three miles away and then a difficult track down the cliff side to the beach would have to be negotiated. The cargo would have to be

7

carried up this track to the cliff top and then to the nearest point to which the horses could be led.

So a further gang would be organised who would gather on the beach to do the carrying. If the cargo were brandy, each man would carry two barrels, one on his back and one on his chest. Some of the more substantial bundles would be hauled up the cliff side by rope. Everything would then be loaded on to the mules or horses and taken to a safe place. This 'safe place' would often be the cellar of an inn, or a house with a false wall in the attic. If the house belonged to someone who was beyond the suspicion of the excise men, so much the better. Another favourite place was the local church tower. In one case, a false floor had been built in between the ringing chamber and the bell chamber and there are local tales about tunnels being built from some churches down to the beach, but there does not seem to be any evidence that this was so. No doubt the parson in these churches received payment in kind, but the men who took part in the actual recovery from the beach and transported it inland could earn more in one night than they could earn in a week of legitimate employment.

But before any of these plans could be put into action, there had to be money available. Suppliers on the continent were not likely to release cargoes of brandy, silks, tobacco, stockings and other desirable commodities without payment. The skipper of the boat involved in the carriage of these goods would need paying. Certain 'payments' might have to be made either for information regarding the movement of customs men or as an inducement for eyes to look the other way. And therefore, in addition to the groups already described, one more man was essential — 'the venturer'. He was the man who found the capital for the operation; the one who took all the financial risks but few of the physical ones, because he remained anonymous. As a local land owner and a man of substance — perhaps even a magistrate, this was natural.

Towards the end of the 18th century the manner of financing smuggling exploits changed. The practice of a single financier went out of favour and more often a group of people would decide on the nature of the cargo they wanted to run and each take out as many shares as they wished to cover the cost. For example, it is reported that £2 would be paid for each tub of brandy. £1 of this would pay for the brandy and £1 would be banked. When the brandy was landed the banked money would pay for the groups supporting the enterprise — the landing and transportation groups, the look outs, and of course the payments for information. If the excise men intervened and the cargo was lost, the £1 banked stayed in the bank, in the case of a successful landing, the investor would make at least 100% profit.

Smuggling had been practised for many centuries — at least since the beginning of the 14th century, and in 1718 an attempt was made to bring it under control with the introduction of The Hovering Act. Under this Act, any vessel operating outside its licensed area was liable to be seized. In 1784, Prime Minister Pitt amended the law to apply to any vessel under sixty tons and which was carrying brandy, tea, wine, coffee or French silk found hovering within three miles of the coast. In an attempt to stop the transfer of smuggled goods from the larger vessel to the shore by rowing boat, any boat with more than four oars was included in the Act, and if such a boat were to be found on the beach it could be cut into three. New, heavier penalties were introduced both for smugglers and also for those who assisted them. Those found signalling from the shore could be sentenced to one month's hard labour. A receiver of smuggled goods could be sentenced to three months in prison and anyone caught smuggling could be transported for seven years. The effect was that people took greater care, and smuggling increased.

Inducements were given to smugglers to turn informer and those who did were pardoned. This advertisement appeared in a newspaper of the time *The Exeter Flying Post*:

### WHITEHALL, October 5, 1791

*Whereas it has been represented to the Commissioners of his Majesty's Customs, that on Tuesday the 16th August last, the DOLPHIN Revenue Cutter, Rich. John, Commander, stationed at the Port of St Ives, fell with a large armed Smuggling Lugger near Padstow in the County of Cornwall, when the Smugglers feloniously fired a shot at the Dolphin, brought her to, and immediately ordered Mr Osmond, the Mate of the Cutter, on board, who found her navigated with about fifty men, all armed and ready for Action, having eight Six-pounders mounted, with as many more in the Hold, and pierced for eighteen Guns.*

*His Majesty, for the better discovering and bringing to Justice the Persons concerned in this Felony and Outrage, is hereby pleased to promise his most gracious Pardon to any one or more of the said Offenders who shall discover his or their Accomplice or Accomplices there, (except the Master or Commander of the said Lugger, or the Person who actually fired) so that one or more of them may be apprehended and convicted of the said offence.*

### HENRY DUNDAS
Customs-House, London. Oct 5, 1791.

It has not been recorded how many took up this offer, but the fact that they lived in a close knit community, and one that looked after its own, had its influence upon whether they should inform or not.

Towards the end of the 18th century, the Revenue Service was beginning to show signs of greater success in preventive work and in apprehending the law breakers. Before this, despite best efforts, the organisation was less sophisticated. During the 16th century attempts were made to deter smugglers, and by the 17th century the Board of Customs had appointed officers to certain ports and the export and import of taxed goods was restricted to specific ports.

In the South Hams, officers were based at Plymouth, to cover the coast eastwards towards Salcombe. There were officers at Salcombe to patrol westwards to meet up with the Plymouth officers, and also eastwards towards Dartmouth. Officers based at Dartmouth would patrol westwards as far as the Salcombe officers' area. Together with a detachment of Dragoons based at Kingsbridge, and who could be called upon to assist, it would have appeared extremely difficult for successful smuggling operations to be carried out. However, two things must be considered.

First, the distance along the coast path from Salcombe to Dartmouth Castle is seventeen miles. The Board of Customs had many of their officers on horseback. However, this stretch of coastline is unsuitable in many areas for horses, and patrols were still made on foot. This means that even on horse back, a message from, say, Prawle Point to the garrison at Kingsbridge would take an hour. On foot it would probably take three times that long. By the time the dragoons had been mobilised and were on their way, the smugglers would have been long gone.

Another important factor to be considered was public opinion. It has been estimated that in the middle of the 18th century fifty per cent of all spirits consumed in Britain were smuggled. It seems to be logical therefore, that people saw no reason to support a system which meant they would have to pay twice as much for their drink, tea, tobacco and other luxuries than had previously been the case. The local landowners and other wealthy people who invested in the trade were also in danger of losing what could be substantial profits. The effect of the increased regulation was inevitably a greater determination to maintain the service offered by the smuggling fraternity.

But in the South Hams this also had a downside. Up to now the 'free-trading' had been conducted with relatively little violence and loss of life. In other parts of Britain, particularly in the south east, the smuggling gangs had been extremely aggressive and battles had taken place with the revenue men. This practice started to creep into Devon. Smugglers added pistols and muskets to their armoury in their efforts to remain free from capture. In turn, the government increased its efforts to deter the 'free traders' activity.

In 1809 the Preventive Water Guard was formed. Watch Houses were built around the coast to keep a constant alert. One of these houses is shown, on a map of 1827, to be situated on the coast south of East Prawle and about one mile east of Prawle Point *(Map Ref. SX783354)*. In addition, Revenue boats patrolled an allocated stretch of coast each night. These were fast, clinker built cutters and were armed with several cannon. Two were based at Plymouth — the Ranger and the Wasp, with forty-one crew members, and the Spider based at Dartmouth with a crew of twenty eight. Now the Revenue Service began to get the upper hand as illustrated by a report in the *Exeter Flying Post* dated 28th January 1819:

*"His Majesty's Revenue Cutter Vigilant arrived at Dartmouth on Thursday last having suffered much and having been at sea during the late gales. The vessel made the following seizures since she has been commanded by Lieutenant Miller, viz: five cutters, three luggers, ten boats, thirty four Englishmen, a great number of foreigners and upwards of 3,000 tubs."* (A tub would have held about four gallons of spirit.) But enough of the end-times — back to smuggling in the South Hams.

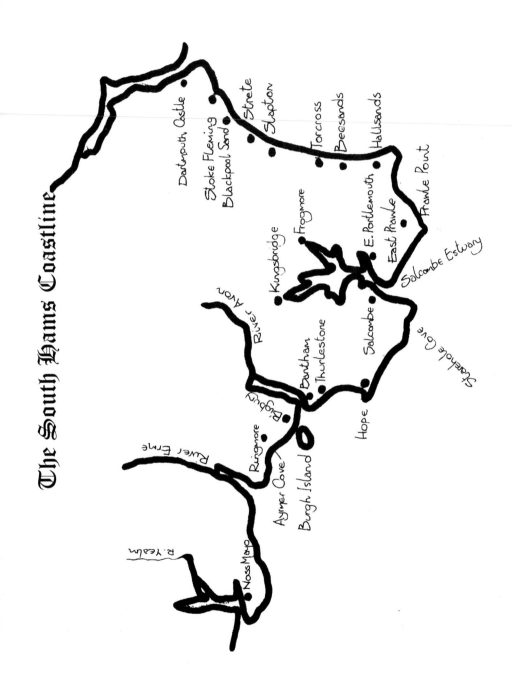

# The South Hams Coastline

Dartmouth Castle
Stoke Fleming
Blackpool Sand
Strete
Slapton
Torcross
Beesands
Hallsands
Frawle Point
E. Portlemouth
East Prawle
Salcombe Estuary
Kingsbridge
Frogmore
Salcombe
Starehole Cove
River Avon
Bantham
Thurlestone
Hope
Bigbury
Ringmore
Aymer Cove
Burgh Island
River Erme
Noss Mayo
R. Yealm

# 5    COVES AND CAVES
## (Dartmouth Castle to Salcombe Estuary)

The landing of smuggled goods from a boat required a beach or cove which was secluded, preferably with somewhere to temporarily store the goods — a cave or a deep cleft — access to the cliff top which was not too difficult, and fairly close proximity to a safe hiding place. It was also desirable that the beach or cove should be a reasonable distance from a centre of administration. These requirements are both fundamental and obvious, but they mean that when we consider possible sites for research into smuggling they help to sort out the possibles from the probables.

Starting at Dartmouth Castle and travelling west, the first possible is **Compass Cove** *(SX884493)*. There is reasonable access to the cliff path, but there is also reasonable and swift access for the Revenue men from Dartmouth. In addition, immediate and safe hiding places do not seem to be available. So, Compass Cove is a doubtful option in spite of there being some local tradition, and legend that it was used as a landing site.

Just over a mile along the coast to the west is **Redlap Cove** *(SX873485)*. This is certainly further away from Dartmouth, and who knows whether or not the owners of Redlap House, just a few hundred yards north of the cove, were sympathetic to the smuggler's cause? There are no records of smuggling activity in the cove, but that only means no one was caught in the act and no history has been handed down verbally.

A further mile west is **Leonard's Cove** *(SX865482)*. This is a different proposition altogether. It is well known, although the facts are mainly anecdotal, that Leonard's Cove was a hive of smuggling activity. Access to the cove is not easy although, until recently, a rope was provided to make it possible for the more agile to reach the beach. At the bottom of the cliffs there is a cave system which has four entrances and would have made ideal storage for contraband. Problems would have been encountered in transferring goods from the beach to the cliff top, but these were by no means insurmountable.

It has long been thought that a tunnel connected the church building at Stoke Fleming to the beach. Recent evidence however, suggests that this was not so. It is now strongly believed that, in fact, a tunnel did exist, but ran from the cellar of the Green Dragon Inn, a 12th century watering hole, to a field below the church, and from there to the cliff top. This tunnel has now collapsed. It is thought that cargoes would be transported along the tunnel and either taken into the church where they would be stored in the tower, or along the next section of the tunnel to the Green Dragon which would either provide storage or a point of sale. It can be seen that Leonard's Cove would have been ideal for the 'free traders' purposes. The cove is secluded. Because the entrance to the tunnel was immediately above the cove, large numbers of men and animals were unnecessary and so discovery and betrayal were less likely, and safe storage was only a short distance away.

Also, because the road is some distance from the cliff top and the land sloping away from the road provides natural cover, men could work on the cliff top undetected — unless of course the law enforcers came in from the sea or took the trouble to walk or ride through the fields towards the beach.

*Green Dragon Inn*

To make a general point: churches were frequently used to store smuggled goods, sometimes with the knowledge of the clergyman, sometimes without. It is said that one church in the South Hams had a false ceiling above the bell ringing chamber, so providing a space between the ringing chamber and the floor of the bell

*Stoke Fleming Church*

chamber. It must have been known by the Revenue men that this practice went on and the question is raised as to why the church authorities seemed to escape detection. Perhaps the Revenue men and the soldiers assisting them were unwilling to have a confrontation with the clergy and the established church.

Travel three quarters of a mile further west and you come to **Blackpool Sands**. It is said that this delightful beach was used by smugglers, but considering the proximity of Leonard's Cove and its superior facilities, there would seem little reason for Blackpool Sands to be involved. Added to that, gangs jealously guarded their own areas and would not have welcomed competition so close at hand. The extra activity may well have alerted the authorities and there was a greater possibility of informants passing information to the excise men. So, apart from

4

Blackpool being used in an emergency by the Stoke Fleming men, the submission is that this is only categorised as a possible site.

The coast now heads south and after two miles is the three mile stretch of **Slapton Sands**. This is a very open stretch of beach, and any movement by day or the glimmer of light by night would easily be seen from one end of the beach to the other. It would also be a difficult beach to escape from in the event of an ambush. At the northern end is the road to Dartmouth and at the southern end the road to Kingsbridge. Both these roads would be used by the militia and the

Revenue men. On the west side of the beach is the Ley. This is a fresh water lagoon surrounded by marshland and would prove disastrous in an escape attempt. There would have been a lane leading to Slapton — where the present road is — but this would be easily blocked. An unlikely smuggling venue, definitely only a possible.

*Torcross and Slapton Sands*

At the southern end of Slapton Sands is the village of **Torcross**. Walk to the end of the sea defence road and climb the steps to the left of the Torcross Hotel. Take the path at the top of the steps until it widens out, and turn left, following the garden wall through a narrow entry way to some more steps. These take you down to Bee Sands. Cross over the top of a culvert exit — this is the overflow from Slapton Ley — and walk along the beach. The headland in front of you is Dun Point. As you approach the end of the line of cliffs, you will see a narrow cleft in the rock face. This is the entrance to Beesands Quarry. The quarry has long been redundant, but is still interesting in its own right. It is almost completely filled with foliage of many kinds and is turning into a sanctuary for birds, mammals and reptiles.

One or two locals however, claim rather hopefully, that it was also a storage place for smuggled goods, which were then carried up the path which leads from the beach on the southern side of the quarry. If this is true, then we have to ask where it was bound for. The nearest house is Widdicombe House, about three quarters of a mile west of the quarry. But this is a grand house and it seems unlikely that the owner would have wished to be involved in such activities. The village of Beeson, about a mile south west, seems a more likely hiding place. But if smuggling really did take place here, it would not have been on a large

15

scale. Rather an activity to supplement the earnings made by the many fishermen working along this stretch of coast.

This theory is supported by a walk further along the beach to the village of Beesands. A little way past the entrance to the quarry, as you pass the end of the cliff system, there is a house called Sunnydale tucked into the hillside. This area is generally known as The Cellars. Here, the fishermen would have had stores, workshops, drying facilities and fish cellars where the pilchard harvest would have been processed, salted, barrelled and transported. Pilchards were caught from spring to autumn, the work was hard and constant and there would have been little time for a second occupation. During the winter the pilchards moved to warmer waters and although other fish would have been caught, it is just conceivable that smuggling might have been a temptation.

However, few, if any, of the fishermen lived in Beesands village. This area was frequently raided by pirates and other opportunist raiders, and for their own protection the fishermen lived in the village of Beeson. If they were afraid to live on the coast, would they have ventured to sea in small boats laden with valuable cargoes of contraband? Another factor — if there is any inkling of smuggling in an area, the local people will claim it almost proudly. After all, it brings in the tourists. In Beesands, apart from the rather vague rumour about activity in the quarry, local people say they have no knowledge of any such trade having been carried out. So let's move on.

Go to the southern end of Beesands village, and a path leads up behind some cottages along the contour of the hill. This is certainly an ancient pathway, and it is tempting to think that it would have been used for nefarious purposes, as maybe it was. But it leads from one remote location, Beesands, to another even more remote location, Start Point. On the way it passes, in about one mile, the village of **North Hallsands** *(SX818387)*. North Hallsands is widely known as a scuba diving centre, and until the hotel recently became derelict, it ran courses in the sport. But, like Beesands, there are not even rumours of smuggling in the vicinity.

Follow the coast path signs and a mile further on is **South Hallsands**. In 1918 the village collapsed into the sea after a storm and is now closed to visitors. But there is much more to the story than that and a visit to the observation platform built above the village is well worth while and where you will be able to read something of the village's history. Perhaps disappointingly, the history does not include smuggling. Disappointing, because of all the villages visited, this one has just the right atmosphere.

Following the coastal path for a further mile, you arrive in Start Point car park. The tarmac road through the white gate leads to the lighthouse.

The coastline now turns west and the first beach offering a safe landing place is **Great Mattiscombe Sand** *(SX816369)*. Again, this is an unlikely smuggling site. It is an open beach where any activity would be observed and it is much more remote than beaches and coves further west where there would be better cover and closer access to storage.

A short distance along the coast is such a beach — **Lannacombe** *(SX802371)* It is relatively secluded with a safe approach and good access to the interior. Three quarters of a mile along the valley which leads out of Lannacombe is South Allington House, and whilst no suggestion is made about the house's involvement in smuggling, it is a house with a long and very interesting history perhaps worth further attention. More directly north is the village of Kellaton *(SX802394)*. Again, there is no evidence of 'free trading', but it would have been a convenient stopping off place and a visit to the village is enough to convince that much has happened there in its ancient past.

Travelling west from here, the coast soon becomes flat and too easily supervised for any suspicious movements to go unobserved, and the rugged terrain does not return for about two miles and until **Prawle Point** *(SX772349)* is reached. In chapter 4, reference was made to a Watch House being built a mile east of Prawle Point as a deterrent to smuggling. But this was not built until the beginning of the 19th century, and whilst these houses did reduce the amount of illegal

*Maceley Cove*

activity after then, this particular house would have only had sight of the very flat area of coastline from Woodcombe Point to Prawle Point. Even before that however, the favoured coves for bringing contraband ashore were on the western side of the point.

**Elender Cove** *(SX768356)* and its near neighbour **Maceley Cove** *(SX766357)* are ideally suited for the trade of the 'gentlemen'. Maceley Cove is not named on Ordnance Survey maps but is the cove nestling against the eastern flank of Gammon Head. Both these coves have steep paths giving access to the beach — Maceley is the less difficult — and both have caves, although at high tide, water does enter these caves. One disadvantage to Elender Cove is that with certain weather and tide conditions, a heavy swell is created which would make landing less safe than on Maceley Cove.

An added advantage to both these coves over others in the area is that it would not have been difficult for horses or mules to be taken to the path above the coves together with as many men as necessary to transport goods from the beach. Old pathways, which still exist, led up the hillside and inland to the village of **East Prawle** *(SX781365)* where, legend has it, The Pig's Nose Inn would offer both storage and disposal. Another attraction for using both the coves and the village is that they are sufficiently distant from the Revenue men based at Salcombe and Dartmouth and the Dragoons at Kingsbridge to give a

*Abraham's Hole, Seacombe Sand*

breathing space for disposal of the goods and escape even after the alarm had been given. A high probability therefore that both Elender Cove and Maceley Coves were used for bringing smuggled goods ashore and that the Pig's Nose Inn was used for receiving them.

The next beach to consider is one and a half miles nearer to Salcombe. This beach has had various names over the years, but is now known as **Seacombe Sand** *(SX754368)*. The beach is easier to get to than any of the other coves or beaches we have considered so far. It usually would offer a safe landing, although quite often there is surf running. There are two factors which make this beach a likely contender for smuggling activity. One is that it has a cave which is named Abraham's Hole. Naming a cave is not unknown, but it is unusual, suggesting that someone named Abraham took a close personal interest in it. Why should a cave be personally associated with someone unless it was being used for nefarious purposes?

The second factor is that there are records of a storage place for smuggled goods in the area and convenient for Seacombe Sand. This is **East Portlemouth Church** *(SX748384)* where the goods were hidden in the tower. In the 18th century it would have been necessary to make a short journey across fields and then down a lane to the churchyard. An early 19th century map shows that there were more roads in the area - one which perhaps led to the beach itself. This would obviously have made the journey more risky, but a short distance along the coast path is a footpath through the bracken which leads to what is obviously an ancient packhorse road, which in turn leads to a rough track into the hamlet of Rickham, so again to the churchyard.

It is often wondered why the church at East Portlemouth is earlier in date than most of the houses in the village. There were at one time two inns in Portlemouth and they were described as hot beds of smuggling. The villagers also were unwilling to work for the estate of the Duke and Duchess of Cleveland who owned all the village and surrounding lands, when they could earn so much more money smuggling. And so, in 1879 the Duke ordered most of the village to be demolished and the people evicted. Therefore, almost all the houses were built in the late 19th or during the 20th century.

We have now reached the Salcombe Estuary. Follow the coast path past Mill Bay and along a road for a quarter of a mile and you come to the ferry.

## 6   COVES AND CAVES
### (Salcombe Estuary to the River Yealm)

The Salcombe Estuary provides the approximate half way point along the South Hams coastline between Dartmouth Castle and the River Yealm. It also provides access to Kingsbridge. In addition, South Pool, West Charleton and

*Frogmore Creek*

Frogmore can be reached along creeks leading off the main estuary although these creeks are tidal. Therefore, if any of the villages near to the water had been considered as possible venues for smuggling, care would have to be taken to avoid being stranded and caught red handed. There are however, down both South Pool and Frogmore Creeks, remains of large lime kilns, and it is known that quite large vessels sailed up these creeks to collect the lime produced. To quote White's Directory of 1878 with regard to Frogmore:

> '*Here are lime kilns, granaries, and coal wharves where vessels of 100 tons load and unload their cargoes.*'

So during the 18th and 19th centuries, navigation must have been safer and easier than it is today. Or perhaps the channels were dredged, and silting up occurred when dredging stopped at the end of the lime trade.

It must be a possibility that contraband was carried inland by these waterways although there is no direct evidence, or even local legend that this happened. It has to be said that the Millbrook Inn at South Pool is an ideal candidate for this trade both by location and atmosphere but again, sadly, there is not an item of confirmation.

Despite the presence of Revenue Officers being stationed at Salcombe, it is known that the town was regularly used for the storage and disposal of illicit cargoes. Once again the church tower was one of the hiding places. The two most likely places for landing these cargoes is **South Sands** *(SX728377)* and **Starehole Cove** *(SX726364)*. Of these, Starehole Cove would have been the safer since it has the advantage of being remote and any activity in the cove could only be observed from one or two isolated viewpoints. The disadvantages would have been the extra distance from Salcombe and the relatively difficult transportation from the beach. On the other hand, despite its close proximity to Salcombe, South Sands is also visible from most angles and any boats approaching the beach would be easily seen by day and blocked by Revenue boats at any time. But as there were excise men stationed in Salcombe, the question arises as to why the town was chosen to be a depot for contraband in the first place.

It is suggested in some records that at least one of the Revenue Officers at Salcombe was in league with the smugglers and in addition to accepting financial inducements from the organisers to turn a blind eye, he took an active part in the proceedings. It must have been a difficult part of the coast to police, so perhaps he operated on the basis of 'If you can't beat them, join them'. Perhaps this is part of the answer to the question 'Why Salcombe?'

The next two miles or so of coastline do not make access from the sea easy because of high cliffs. Although just beyond Bolberry Down there is a cave named **Hugh's Hole** *(SX680386)*. This raises again the question as to why a cave should bear the name of someone unless it has been used for smuggling.

**Hope Cove** *(SX674398)* is a probable site worthy of consideration, if only

*Hope Cove*

because it has the right ambience. But it has more than that. It is remote even today, but in the 18th and 19th centuries it is reported that the road from Malborough to Hope was in such bad condition that it was dangerous to drive there. Hope is also far enough away from both Salcombe and Plymouth to mean a delay in the arrival of the Revenue men. It is suggested that the majority of Hope Cove fishermen were involved in the trade of smuggling and, because of the organisation necessary, that would mean the families of the fishermen and the rest of the community also.

Legend has it that there is a cottage near Shippen Rock which had a trap door leading to a tunnel, which led to a cave on the beach. The landward side of the tunnel collapsed some time ago, but until fairly recently there was a passage leading from the entrance to the cave for some thirty to forty yards, suggesting that there is some truth in the legend. A further rock fall has blocked even this and the entrance now extends for only a few yards.

If you take the road east towards Galmpton, there is an old cottage named Smugglers End, which is also reputed to have been a hiding place for smuggled goods.

Hope Cove is one of only a few places where names of local smugglers are recorded. Although probably most of the village supplemented their meagre incomes with 'fair trading', it would seem that two brothers, Richard and Philip Kingcup, were the ring leaders. It is recorded that Philip was drowned at sea, but the circumstances of his demise are not clear.

Follow the coast path for two miles and you come to the long stretch of beach shown as **Thurlestone Sand** on the Ordnance Survey maps *(SX676415)*, but known as Yarmer Sands by the locals. This is an unobstructed and sheltered beach and offers a good landing place for small boats. It is also, even today, quite remote; the nearest main road being some five miles away. So unless an excise man happened to be passing, it is a beach which would have lent itself well for bringing smuggled goods ashore. Add to that the close proximity of the village of Thurlestone and the possibility of good storage facilities and you have an excellent location.

*Thurlestone Church Porch*

In Thurlestone, the church building was again a hiding place. It is recorded that on occasions as many as fifty barrels of spirits would be hidden on the roof of the church porch. Most of the time this would have been with the connivance of the Rector, who no doubt received his 'brandy for the parson' in return. However, when the Reverend Peregrine Ilbert was appointed to the parish in 1839 he preached hell fire sermons against the practice of smuggling, oblivious of the fact that booty was still being hidden behind the castellations on the porch roof.

Take the path which skirts the golf course and in a further two miles you will arrive at the surfer's paradise of **Bantham**. This was a favourite landing place for smuggled goods and the home of a notorious smuggler, Nat Cleverly. Cleverly was the owner of a large fishing boat, and made frequent and regular trips to Roscoff to collect the goods which made him both a wealthy and influential man. The Revenue men were determined to catch him and make him an example and he became the target of their attention. At one point things were so difficult for Cleverly that he gave himself up. He appeared before the magistrate, who happened to be one of his good customers and was found not guilty and released. The next day he was back in Roscoff making his purchases and preparing for another run to Bantham.

*River Avon, Bantham*

Anecdotal evidence would suggest that in addition to much of the village being involved in smuggling, equally, much of the village was a hiding place for incoming goods. Most of the cottages would have had a secret hiding place and the rewards to those who offered their services in this direction or in bringing the goods ashore would have assured people like Cleverly of their absolute loyalty. As a result, the community became so close knit that it would have been most unlikely for anyone to inform the authorities for fear of retribution.

There are a number of questions remaining about Bantham, one of them being, what part did the Sloop Inn play in the communal activity. As far as can be ascertained, although the building itself has been there for a long time — perhaps since the 1400s, it was not an inn until the latter part of the 19th century when a special ale, local to the area was brewed at the back of

*Bantham Village*

the inn. It may have been a farm during the period we are considering and it is difficult to believe that the owners would not have played some part in the profit making community enterprise.

Another notorious character operating out of Bantham was Tom Crocker, although he based himself on **Burgh Island** *(SX647439)*. Tom is mainly a man of fable. Little or nothing is known of him although numerous stories surround him. Most of these however have been passed down verbally through the generations and although there is no doubt a basis of truth in them, much of the fact has been lost in the transmission. There are, for example, no reports of his

23

activities in the newspaper *The Exeter Flying Post,* neither are there any reports in the court records of the time. One of the difficulties is that although it is

*Burgh Island*

believed that he was shot by Revenue men on August 14th, no one seems to know which year. This does not make investigation easy. There is little doubt though that someone named Tom Crocker used Burgh Island as a base for smuggling. One thing is certain, Burgh Island is the most atmospheric location in the whole of the South Hams and it is a place that must be visited. If this is what you wish, the first thing you have to do is get to **Bigbury on Sea** *(SX653445).* If you are walking and you have got as far as Bantham, you need to cross the Avon. If the tide is in there is a ferry, depending on the season. This is sign posted from the car park booth. Alternatively, you have to get to Aveton Gifford roundabout *(SX692473),* and walk back along the tidal road. But as this adds ten or more miles to your journey, it might be wiser to make more suitable travel arrangements before you start or to wait for the tide to go down. At low tide it is possible, given the right conditions, to wade the Avon from *SX667437.* But great care must be taken and ideally this should only be attempted in calm conditions and at low spring tide.

*The Pilchard Inn*

On arrival at Bigbury on Sea, cross the car park and go down the slipway to the shore. If the tide is out a causeway makes it possible to walk to the island. Otherwise you may cross on a specially designed tractor which runs a half hourly service.

On the quay is the Pilchard Inn. This goes back to 1336 and was almost certainly Tom Crocker's retreat and storage place. If you walk up the hill past the porch of the inn — where Crocker is said to have been shot — you come to a gate. Follow the lower path and almost at the cliff top, follow the path to the right to some ancient steps which lead down to a beach at low tide. Turn left into the cove and you will find Tom Crocker's Cave. There was at some time, a tunnel which led from this cave to the cellar of the Pilchard Inn, but both ends have now been bricked up.

Trading — apart from 'free trading' — has been part of Burgh Island's history since the Bronze Age, and the history of the island is fascinating, but this has nothing to do with smuggling. So further information may be found in *Appendix 1*.

Following the coast path westward, the next community to be encountered is **Challaborough** *(SX648448)*. You would be forgiven for believing that it would not have been in existence as a community before the invention of the caravan. There must be hundreds of residential caravans laid out in the valley with military precision. Some of them are permanently occupied, but the majority are holiday lets, as are many of the *Tom Crocker's Cave*

houses which surround them. Yet there was a fishing community here at one time. It is not though a place which would appear to have any involvement in pre-1850's smuggling.

*Ayrmar Cove*

From the west end of the coast road a narrow track can be found between a garage and a bungalow which climbs up to the cliff top. In about half a mile the path descends into **Ayrmar Cove** *(SX641455)*. Ayrmar Cove immediately gives the impression of being an ideal smuggling venue. The approach from the sea is safe and relatively free from rocks, and the landing is on a gently sloping beach. A narrow, sheltered track leads up from the beach to the village of **Ringmore** *(SX653458)*. It is easy to imagine the village being able to offer safe storage for contraband in either its ancient buildings, the church or more probably the Journeys' End Inn. The inn dates from the late part of the 13th century and it is said that it was built to house the masons who

were building the church in the village. The inn is large and complex, and could probably even now hide a cargo of contraband quite successfully. Legend has it that a tunnel was built between the inn and the beach, but as in many such cases, this is not likely. The cove is almost three quarters of a mile from the inn and it would be a formidable task to build a tunnel

*Journeys' End Inn*

for that distance, especially as the trackway leading up from the beach is perfectly adequate for pack mules or ponies to carry the landed goods.

Strangely, in such an ideal situation, there are no stories told about smuggling days. Talking to the local historian does not throw any light on the subject and even the owner of the inn does not make any claims other than to point out a room behind the fireplace in the bar where smugglers would gather. If you go out of the front door of the inn, turn right and walk up the hill, you will find at the top of the hill the almost inevitable 'Smuggler's Cottage'. In this case however, apart from being the right age, you get the feeling that it might just have a ring of truth about it. There is one added bonus. On the western side of the beach there is a large cave which can be reached at low tide. It is surely certain that there was smuggling here.

Returning to the coast path and travelling west brings you, after a steep climb and an equally steep descent, to **Westcombe Beach** *(SX634458)*. It is possible to argue that any of the coves and beaches along this stretch of coast may have been used for smuggling, but with several ideal landing places just a little to the east, Westcombe seems unlikely.

The walk from here to the River Erme is painfully steep and brings nothing in terms of evidence of smuggling or even suitable coves and it is a relief to reach the level ground of the Erme Estuary for a rest.

First impressions would suggest that the Erme would seem to be a first class passage inland for contraband. Even at low tide it would be possible to proceed for some distance in a shallow draft boat. The disadvantage would have been that there was no possibility of taking evasive action should the Preventive men arrive on the scene. Progress would be slow and they would only have to throw

26

a net across the river to create a trap. But who knows for certain? The true significance of the Erme lies much further back in history. *(See Appendix 3)* The River Erme now presents a problem. To continue on foot either necessitates a diversion of something like a seven miles round trip to reach the nearest road

bridge or a degree of patience whilst waiting for the tide to go out. For about an hour or so on either side of low tide, the river can be waded, though care should be taken. The best route is the shortest route to reach the slip way which can be seen on the opposite shore *(SX614478)*. Walk up the slip and follow the obvious coast path.

*River Erme*

This is the final leg of the journey. If you have walked this far out of an interest in smuggling in the South Hams before 1850, you ought to know that there is no evidence from this point to Noss Mayo, our final destination, and you may decide that enough is enough. You may also wonder why this information was not disclosed before the crossing of the Erme. The answer to that is simple. Now you are on the western bank of the river, you might as well carry on to the end. Apart from a couple of steep sections at the start of this stretch, it is, with one exception, comfortable walking, the views are magnificent and there are one or two items of interest on the way.

After a mile and a half you will come to a rocky pillar. This is **St Anchorites Rock** *(SX592472)*. The name is said to have come from a hermit who once spent his days perched on top of the pinnacle. A short distance to the west there are several caves cutting into the cliff, but access is difficult and they are unlikely to have been used for storing contraband.

The path follows the contour of the hill for just over a mile after which it drops down towards **Ivy Cove** *(SX576466)*. The hill ahead is the exception to comfortable walking, but struggle on and you arrive at **Beacon Hill** *(SX573468)*. Records show that the ruined building on Beacon Hill is known as Membland Pleasure House. One thing that the records do not show is what sort of pleasure the building provided. One writer suggests diplomatically that it was a tea house. This is quite possible because it is at this point that **Revelstoke Drive** becomes a feature and the walking becomes a gentle stroll. Revelstoke Drive is an old carriageway which can be followed almost into Noss Mayo and is a massive civil engineering project. Especially so when it is realised that it was constructed by unemployed fishermen with simple hand tools. Lord Revelstoke's original intention was to build a footpath to impress his guests, but when it was completed,

he inspected it and decided that it should be three feet wider so that it could be negotiated by carriages. It is a remarkable achievement.

Following the drive westward you arrive, after about one mile, at **Stoke House** *(SX562468)*. You can, if you wish, cross the car park ahead and continue along the drive. It is worth however, turning left and

*Revelstoke Drive*

walking down the hill through the caravan site to the ancient church of St Peter the Poor Fisherman. It is said that parts of the building are Saxon, but earliest records seem to be 13th century. It used to be the parish church for Noss Mayo despite the village being a mile and a half away. In 1840 the church was badly damaged by storms and after Lord Revelstoke built another church in Noss Mayo it was abandoned. It is now maintained by the Redundant Churches Fund and a dedicated band of volunteers. It is still a

*St. Peter the Poor Fisherman*

dedicated building and occasional services are held there.

Instead of retracing the path up the hill, take the footpath through the woods and along the cliff top. After half a mile follow the path up a steep hill and rejoin the carriageway. It is now a pleasant walk of three and a half miles to Noss Mayo where two very good inns will provide refreshment — but not, unfortunately, evidence of smuggling.

We started our journey along the coast path through the South Hams at Dartmouth Castle looking for evidence of smuggling in the 18th and 19th centuries. The question has to be — have we found it? If we were hoping for irrefutable, recorded evidence, the answer has to be — probably not. But as previously there were only two or maybe three cursory, almost passing references to such activities in the area, it can now be argued that there is ample anecdotal and some circumstantial evidence that smuggling was rife in more places than was once suspected.

*Noss Mayo*

Walk through villages like Stoke Fleming, Strete, Hope Cove, Kellaton and Ringmore, and talk to the older residents in the inns and you will feel the atmosphere and know that the old aural tradition is still active. A man in his eighties in Hope Cove for instance, remembering tales told by his grandmother of the 'free-traders' passing the house in dead of night leading many laden ponies with sacking muffling their hooves. Maybe his tongue was loosened by a pint of ale, but there was an insistence that rang true. Read John Masefield's book '*Jim Davis*'. Yes, of course it is a novel, but it fits so well with the facts that are related as you walk this remote coast path.

If you complete the walk and are still not convinced that boats were drawn up in some of these lonely coves, contraband carried up the cliff path and loaded on to pack ponies and then taken to some safe hiding place before being distributed up-country; if you still do not believe that the very path on which you are walking was once used for this very purpose, but also the one along which the Preventive men gave chase and probably battles were fought, then you have a consolation. You have had a good walk through some of the most beautiful and rugged scenery in the country, and you have had the opportunity to visit welcoming village inns, many of them hundreds of years old, and you have experienced conversations with some very interesting people. But this is not the end. There are two topics which have to be touched on first. One is piracy, another, wrecking but first let's come up to date because smuggling still goes on.

# 7. THE PRESENT DAY

During the later part of the 19th century and the first half of the 20th century the practice of smuggling went through a period of drastic transition. For a number of reasons the Customs and Excise authorities were beginning to take greater control of the situation and it was becoming more and more difficult to successfully land and dispose of contraband. Communications had certainly improved both by land and, with improved boats, by sea; then improved further with the invention of the telephone and radio.

By the 1950s social structures had changed and so had the demands being made on those who were still anxious to make a dubious living by bringing into the country goods which if declared, would be either very expensive, or banned altogether. In our major cities the drug culture was developing and whilst much was home grown, such as cannabis, people were looking for new and more exotic experiences and soon found themselves in the hands of suppliers who, as the trade developed further, found themselves in the hands of the smugglers who in turn became involved in organised crime syndicates quick to see a profit. It became obvious that unless drastic action was taken, matters could easily get completely out of control. The law was strengthened by the imposition of serious penalties for those convicted of smuggling offences, and Her Majesty's Customs and Excise Service became much more sophisticated and effective.

As the 20th century moved into its last quarter, smuggling also became more sophisticated and effective. Looking at it simplistically, smuggling could be said to fall into three main categories: tobacco, drugs and people. A Treasury Department press release in 2001 estimated that one in five cigarettes smoked in the UK are smuggled. In the same year the government committed £209 million over the next three years to tackle smuggling in all its aspects. In addition, new and severe penalties were introduced for those convicted. This shows the degree of concern in the minds of those in authority.

The drug problem is potentially much more serious. Most of the drugs taken by British users come from thousands of miles away. The raw materials for heroin for example may originate in countries in south west Asia, such as Pakistan and Afghanistan. Cocaine most usually originates in South America and a great deal is then routed through the West Indies and either through Europe or directly to the UK by a variety of methods. Because of the involvement of organised crime in the distribution of illegal drugs, and also because of the massive profits involved, extreme violence is often a part of the scene, either threatened or in fact, and the people acting as couriers may be seen simply as disposable systems of transport.

When it is realised that a kilo of heroin costs less than £1,000 in Pakistan but on British streets is worth more than £75,000, it is fairly obvious why some people take such risks in pursuing their potentially lethal trade.

An equally lucrative activity is the smuggling of people. European police forces say that gangs are making as much money from people trafficking as they are from drug smuggling. In July 2001 it was claimed by the German Intelligence Service, BND, that the smuggling of people into the European Union earns an income of more than £3 billion annually. Because of the huge sums involved, this practice is also careless of lives and many people die in the attempt.

All this has, over the last few years, brought about a reorganisation of the Customs and Excise Service and a modernising of their plant and equipment to a highly technical standard. This brings us back from the national situation to the picture in the South Hams of Devon. Over quite a long period of time, the Customs and Excise Service have been rationalising their activities and reducing the small outposts which were once situated in most harbours. The present policy is to have a concentration of resources in major ports and in airports and to react to intelligence for dealing with potential incidents outside these areas. The major port covering the South Hams is Plymouth. And even though this means covering many miles of coastline, it has not meant a dilution of the service; in fact it could be argued that because of technical advances and an improvement in information received the service has benefited.

One such advance is the arrival of a new Customs Cutter in Plymouth. The first Customs Cutter was purchased in 1149 for the sum of £22. The new addition, the 'Seeker', cost £4.5 million. She is forty two metres long and carries a crew of twelve and is one of a highly successful class of fast patrol boats fitted with the most up to date navigation and surveillance equipment. In spite of this, customs officers would admit that some of the remote coves used by the smugglers of two hundred years ago might still be used. It is not unknown for example for an unrecognised yacht to dump a cargo of drugs overboard off a lonely beach to be recovered later. Officers would also admit that only three or four arrests have been made for serious smuggling offences in the South Hams in the ten years from 1993 to 2003. Perhaps the system of deterrent is working.

31

At first sight it might be difficult to understand how smuggling and wrecking have much in common, but there are two common factors.  Firstly, smugglers bring undeclared goods ashore illegally for their own use and to sell for profit.

Wreckers do the same. Smugglers however, have paid for their goods, wreckers have not, and in certain circumstances are guilty of theft.  The second common factor is that those people taking part in wrecking are also, more often than not, involved in smuggling.

Much has been written about the practice of wrecking — that is, deliberately luring ships on to dangerous headlands and rocky coasts by the showing of lights from the shore.  It has to be said however, that there is little or no firm evidence that this took place.  It also seems unlikely that men would hold a vigil at night on the coast path showing lights to ships that might or might not pass by when all they had to do was wait until a ship found the rocks with the help of an onshore storm and treacherous currents.  The truth was almost more inhuman than the conjecture.

For many years the law stated that a ship ashore was not a wreck unless no man, dog or cat had survived.  If man, dog or cat did indeed survive a ship running aground, the owners of the ship were to be informed and they had a year and a day to claim the cargo and any other goods to which they had rights.  It would seem very unlikely that anyone so surviving, either members of the crew or passengers, would lay down the law in the face of a fierce looking mob from the local town or village intent on stripping the ship bare and tell them that they were breaking the law.  The fact remains that survivors coming ashore meant that the ship could not be declared a wreck, and anyone removing goods from it was guilty of robbery. Some mobs would just ignore the law and the survivors would be allowed to escape inland, having been frightened out of their wits by threats of violence.  These were the compassionate wreckers.  Others would not show such consideration.

As the law was specific about anything reaching the shore alive, many determined mobs would make absolutely certain that nothing did.  Or at least, if they did make it to the shore alive, they did not remain so for very long.

There was no sentiment, sympathy or mercy shown to the survivors.  The motive of the mob was not only greed, although this was a great part of it.  In the 17th, 18th and early 19th centuries, many families living in communities on or near the coast in rural areas were often leading an impoverished existence to the point that a wreck could mean their survival.  In a way therefore, it could be seen as the survival of the fittest, brutal as that was.

The law needed to be changed. As it was, the wreckers had nothing to lose. If they were apprehended either robbing the grounded ship, or later discovered to be in possession of goods from the ship, penalties were heavy. Hard labour was usual, transportation an alternative and death by hanging was carried out in certain circumstances. If there were no survivors, there were no witnesses and there was the chance of remaining undiscovered. Even if the authorities did find evidence in your house or on your person, the penalties would only be the same as if you had been apprehended in the act of robbing the ship.

The bodies of the victims, either washed ashore from the ship or killed when they arrived, would have been buried on the beach. It was the custom for bodies found on the beach to be buried where they were found and so it was not likely that the evidence would be discovered. Even if bodies were found, the practice of forensic science was unknown, and so, almost certainly the perpetrators would get away with it. An Act of Parliament in 1808 required that any bodies so discovered must be given a Christian burial in consecrated ground. But this presumed that the body had been found by a law abiding member of the community. In 1963 some children digging on the sands at Thurlestone discovered nine skeletons in a mass grave. It was thought probable that they were victims of the wrecking of the Ramillies on February 15th, 1760.

Another Act of Parliament was passed in 1713 'to better protect the fate of vessels in distress and their cargoes'. But this was just more words and was ignored by those for whom wrecking was an accepted and acceptable way of life. Clergy in parishes on or near to the coast were ordered to read this Act to their congregations four times a year and to spell out to them the nature of the penalties which could be imposed for the guilty. This practice tended to prove less effective due to the fact that a number of the clergy were involved in the practice of wrecking themselves.

The story is told that in one South Hams village church the clergyman was half way through his sermon when someone entered the church, approached him in the pulpit and whispered a message. The clergyman came down from aloft, removed his robes, moved to the door and announced, "There's a wreck on the beach. Every man for himself".

Wrecking, that is removing goods from a grounded ship without authority, still goes on today. When a ship laden with timber went aground on a South West beach in 2002, literally thousands of people removed as much of the cargo as they could manage. Even quite large trucks, including a low loader, were driven to the beach to take away whatever they could carry. It appeared to the casual observer, that the police were powerless in the face of so many people. Nothing has changed — except that as from the middle part of the 19th century, treatment of survivors has been more humane.

For several centuries, the South West coast of England was terrorised by raiders from the sea. There were opportunists who landed near a village and stole whatever they could lay their hands on. They were thugs, and like the thugs of today, had no respect for anyone who stood in their way. There were smugglers who supplemented their income with part-time piracy. Tom Crocker of Burgh Island was a man who wore both hats. These people would challenge a boat offshore and take its cargo, or they would lie in wait ashore and steal the cargo as it was unloaded. Sometimes the cargo stolen would have been smuggled goods anyway, and so it was a bit like dog eat dog.

These raiders could create havoc in a community and it was easy to understand why there were very few coastal communities between the 16th and the 18th centuries. People lived in hamlets and villages a mile or two inland as a small deterrent to the robbers. But the raiders who must have created absolute and unimaginable terror were the Barbary Coast pirates, who, from the stories that emerge from the sparse records that exist, created chaos around South Western coasts.

From early in the 17th century there had been rumours that shipping was being attacked in the Western Approaches, around the Mediterranean and off the North African coasts. For some time these rumours were denied, especially by the owners of merchant ships, whose crews were refusing to voyage into these waters. Certainly, ships travelling out to the New World both with cargoes and with new settlers were not arriving at their destinations, and boats which had set off on long fishing expeditions were not returning home. When attacks commenced on villages on the west country coast and whole communities were carried away by raiders, rumours became facts. At this point trade came almost to a standstill. Fishermen and the crews of commercial ships were both in fear of their lives and also unwilling to leave their families to these attacks. At first the authorities said that the navy did not have sufficient ships and manpower to tackle the problem. Then, when the attacks and pleas for help persisted, they told the suffering communities that they were exaggerating the problem. It was soon realised however, that the reports were not exaggerated and that the perpetrators were not ordinary, opportunist raiders, but pirates from the Barbary Coast of North Africa.

These men had one aim in mind — to take people and sell them into slavery. They were authorised by their various governments to attack and take ships of Christian countries, selling the men into slavery and either destroying their boats or taking them as booty. They travelled in fast lateen rigged ships called xebecs, and oared galleys. It seems that they were able to attack as they pleased and it is reported that in one year alone (Some reports claim in two or three days, but this is unlikely), they captured twenty seven ships in the seas around Plymouth. But their raids on land based communities where all the men would be at sea and only women, children and the elderly left must have been absolutely terrifying. Running their ships up on to suitable beaches in the dark they would take whatever and whoever they could find.

There are no records of numbers of people taken in these raids and there are few accounts of anyone returning to give evidence. There are reports of men occasionally wandering around west country towns with their tongues cut out and the ensuing conjecture that they had been victims of torture by the pirates caused even more terror. In some cases ransoms were claimed for those taken, but the victims would not usually be rich enough to buy their freedom. When the captives were brought for sale, usually at the slave market in Algiers, those who had special skills would fare better than the others. For example, a Master Mariner might well be offered employment as a navigator in the very pirate fleet that had captured him. If he agreed, he would have been paid a salary that compared favourably with employment either in the Royal Navy or the merchant service. The alternative was pure slavery, which in turn meant a very uncertain life expectancy. Not much of a choice even for the most loyal person. Those who had no skills would be sold into hard labour where survival was all that mattered. They were fed three loaves of bread a day and because of the nature of the work, the death rate was probably high. The solution was simple — they would be replaced. The women, if suitable would be sold to harems and might well have fared better in terms of accommodation and food.

It might be thought that with so many slaves being employed, there would have been some attempt to escape. There probably was, and certainly some escapes are recorded in documents of the time. But it must be realised that when slaves were taken from the market by the owners, particularly by the Dey or local ruler, they would usually be placed in shackles, and at night would be housed in cells with a dozen or more men in each cell. There was also the deterrent of torture and the painful death to which a runaway slave would be sentenced. Physical mutilation would first be carried out and then the culprit would be subject to one of a number of frightening executions. Decapitation was possibly the most humane. Others would include impalement on hooks protruding from the wall, being nailed to a wooden frame, having lighted candles inserted into open wounds and being burned slowly to death and as many others as the imaginations of the executioners could devise.

There was one more significant torture. The seafarers of the west country were devout Christians and it was believed that capture by the Barbary Coast pirates would lead to eternal damnation. There would be no chance of practising their religion under the conditions in which they were held. There was no contact with a priest or a place of worship where sacraments could be received, and the nearest they would get to God would be through Islam, and this was unthinkable. They truly believed that because they had been removed from the teachings of Christ, all hope of salvation had gone as well. For many, this was as serious as the threatened physical torture.

As the 17th century developed and certainly by the 18th century it was obvious that something had to be done by the authorities. Merchant ships and indeed boats involved in smuggling were arming themselves against attacks by pirates. It is alleged that the Barbary pirates were not determined fighting men, and the raids both on shipping and coastal communities diminished until, by the middle of the 18th century they were virtually unknown. The fear remained however, particularly in the villages, and it was a long time before people slept soundly in their beds.

One of the Barbary pirates ships was wrecked in a storm off Gara Rock, near Salcombe. The ship carried a cargo of gold bullion, gold coins, jewellery and other treasures — obviously the plunder from their victims. Kendall McDonald gives a good account of this wreck in his book '*Shipwrecks of The South Hams*'.

We believe that we live in uncertain times today — and so we do. But it is almost unimaginable to think of living in the poverty, danger and fear that so many had to live with in the 17th, 18th and 19th centuries and what they had to do simply to survive. We should also reflect on the fact that the year 1715 started the 'Age of Enlightenment'.

## Appendix 1    Burgh Island - a brief history.

Tin, mined on Dartmoor and smelted on the moor and on the coast, was brought down the River Erme, when some was shipped out directly by North African traders and the remainder stored on the island awaiting shipment. A Greek merchant named Pytheas knew much about the tin trade, and in the year 325BC he explored the coastal region of Devon and Cornwall, writing this on his return home:

*"The inhabitants of Britain who live in the South-West are especially friendly to strangers and from meeting foreign traders have adopted civilised habits. It is these people who produce the tin, cleverly working the land that bears it. They dig out the ore, melt it and purify it. They then hammer the metal into ingots like knucklebones and transport them to an island off the coast called Ictis, for the channel dries out at low tide and they can take over large quantities on their carts. Merchants purchase the tin from the natives there and ship it back to Gaul".*

Since before the Roman occupation tin ore had been mined on Dartmoor. After the ore had been processed, the tin ingots were brought down to the sea by way of the River Erme and possibly the Avon. The wreck of a Bronze Age ship has been found with a cargo of tin ingots at the mouth of the River Erme, and near to the site of a pre-Roman harbour. *(See Appendix 2)*. The Avon enters the sea on Burgh Island's doorstep, so to speak, and the River Erme flows into the sea only a short distance to the west. Does this relate to the writings of Pytheas?

Up to now this has been, to some extent, conjecture. There is one piece of evidence however that ties in Burgh Island to the Bronze Age without any argument. In the 1930s there was an accidental find of a Bronze Age mould for a palstave — a bronze axe head — and this is now in the possession of the City of Plymouth Museum. It is unfortunate that there has been no further archaeological investigation to look further into the island's history.

Two other islands claim to be the original Isle of Ictis — the Isle of Wight and St Michael's Mount in Cornwall. Pytheas states that the island he identifies as Ictis has a causeway access at low tide. Geologists would argue that the Isle of Wight has not had causeway access to the mainland since Neolithic times, and in Roman times it was known as Vectis. As far as St Michael's Mount is concerned, it is argued that at the time of the visit of Pytheas, the island was five or six miles inland. The strong possibility is therefore, that Burgh Island is the original Ictis.

Burgh Island has almost certainly been occupied for more than two and half thousand years. Little is known of its history from its early trading days until mediaeval times when a monastery was built and dedicated to St Michael and so there would have been the monks in residence and the visiting pilgrims who would probably have lodged at the Pilchard Inn. After this there would have been a time of lawlessness when the island would have been a refuge for pirates, smugglers and others. At some point, probably after the dissolution of the monasteries in 1538, a small chapel was built on the highest point, also dedicated to St Michael. This was later used as a look out (a huer's hut) for fishermen watching for the approach of the pilchard shoals but is now in ruins.

The present hotel was built in 1928 and there is a long list of famous guests who have stayed there including the Duke of Windsor, Noel Coward, Kirk Douglas and Agatha Christie, who wrote several of her books while staying at the hotel, and in at least one, it formed the basis of the story.

*Huer's hut*

*Appendix 2.*
Bronze Age palstave mould found on Burgh Island.
*(Reproduced by permission of Plymouth City Museums & Art Gallery)*

This is a one piece mould; the metal being poured into the mould until level with the top and then, when set, removed, polished, sharpened, and fitted with a haft.

*Appendix 3    The River Erme.*

The River Erme was without doubt an important route inland for goods both into and out the interior, particularly in the days when road access was even worse than it is today. The mouth of the river was also a renowned ships graveyard and there are many wrecks on Mary's Rocks in the mouth of the river. One of these wrecks, or at least its cargo of tin ingots, fairly recently discovered, was a Bronze Age tin trader dating back to 1,000BC. This is extremely significant in terms of the history of this part of the South Hams coast. Together with the discovery of similar ingots and a mould for a palstave dating back to the Bronze Age on Burgh Island, it proves beyond reasonable doubt that the island was connected with tin trading 3,000 years ago. It seems reasonable to suppose that such trading continued into Roman times and therefore that the comments of the trader Pytheas reported in *Appendix 1* support the argument that Burgh Island is the island referred to by Pytheas as Ictis.